Between the Inhale and the Exhale

Jennifer LeRouge

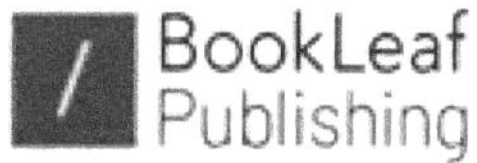
BookLeaf
Publishing

Presentation by *BookLeaf Publishing*

Web: www.bookleafpub.com

E-mail: info@bookleafpub.com

ISBN: 9789357211161

First edition 2022

DEDICATION

For my mom. No one has tried harder to love me, and no one is more deserving of the words "thank you." I hope you get to read this.

ACKNOWLEDGEMENT

Christine LeRouge
David Clewell
Gloria Bruno
Kate Northcott
Jaci Hollenberg
Brandon Steffe
Andrea Gibson

If I Had One Superpower

My superpower would be
Super Sensitivity.
To everything.

I can turn your pauses between words
into lifetimes. Easily.
Whole lives envisioned, but never lived out.
Good and bad.

I'm not sure if anyone else noticed,
but a few years ago,
they changed they yellow in the traffic lights
here
to a perfect lemon yellow.
And now when I get caught at one,
I can't help but smile, even on my worse days.

When you read a good poem
I mean - a really good one -
you may dog-ear the page
so you don't forget.
But I never have to make a crease.
The words move me, change me, every time.
Forgetting just isn't possible.

Yes, the pain can be excruciating.

Even, and often, imaginary.
But not many people fashion a smile
when caught at a traffic light.
But I do.

Once Weight Guesser, Now Poet Laureate

We were the Knights of the Round Table
in the stuffed, paneled poetry workshop glass.
The center of the table littered
with absolute treasures
from writers - warriors - I didn't even know
existed.

You were teaching us that a sharp mind
was the only sure-fire weapon to win the battle,
and that truth was the Holy Grail itself.

You shared the wisdom you acquired throughout
your quest
as a carnival weight guesser,
professional wrestler,
university professor,
and now Poet Laureate
to aid us in our own truth-seeking.

Your class served as a confessional,
therapy session,
underground meeting of revolutionaries,
a safe space for unsafe thinking,
with only one rule:

"Look it up, or die."

The Art of Living

Being isn't always beautiful.
Growling is rarely graceful.
Existing is not constant elegance.

But find a moment in the chaos
to stop and look and feel.
Your work-in-progress
is already a masterpiece.

What I Remember About You

I remember falling asleep in your lap.
So inconvenient for you because you were
always at your computer
trying to get work done.
You'd see me trying to look as sleepy-eyed as
possible,
so I wouldn't get turned down,
and you'd smile your crooked smile and extend
your arms.

I remember defending you
when Shelley would vent
about how you never understood her, and never
tried to.
How you weren't a good dad.
I never let her have the last word.

I remember turning 13,
and getting into our first real argument
about whether I was my sister's 'minion'.
You didn't understand me. And you didn't even
try to.

I remember being 16,

and we got into our worst fight.
which is saying a lot,
as our fights were abundant enough
to fill the dusty office you're never in anymore.
You said I wasn't your daughter in your eyes
anymore
and left for the night.

I remember squeezing your hand
in the hospital room not soon after,
knowing that if you weren't in a coma then,
you wouldn't had let me.

I remember hearing the endless beep
as they turned the machines off,
already having trouble remembering your voice.

Damsel in Distress

I have finally realized
asking for safety
is not the same thing
as asking to be saved.

Question to the Executioner

What should you do
when even "ideal" doesn't seem worth it?
When you come to the decision
that the price tag on "perfect" is just too steep.
When the what if's lasso your hope
until your asking - begging - the executioner
to just get it over with.

The magnolia breeze is sweet,
but there is no sweet
that can touch the bitterness
I've already swallowed.

As the noose is knotted,
I'll exhale easier knowing I really did try.

The Girl in the Pink Bathing Suit

I found myself measuring time
by the rise of the tides.

Peaks of blues and greens
rushing over the jagged rocks
and foaming white
toward the small girl's feet
as she played in the sand.

The lowering sun and rising waters colored
her backdrop
the most beautiful gradient,
which complemented the girl's bathing suit
Folding and bunching
under her carefree movements.

The girl danced
her pink twirl
in the newly golden day.
And I drunk in her beauty
like Degas lost at sea.

Making a Claim

When chance and choice collide,
how do you know who's to blame?
Does it matter
when you're the only one
left at the accident?

My Favorite Painting at NOMA

Based on "Guardian Angels" (1946) Dorothea
Tanning - painting on display at the New
Orleans Museum of Art

I have a recurring dream. Or nightmare?
A surreal scene
of a clouded, dusky sky.
Overlooking my most recent home.
Deployed over ten months ago.

Trunks twisted together like metal during
impact.
Like bodies under fire,
like my face between recognizing
I've killed an enemy
and another human being.

No.
Not clouds.
The strokes of whites and grays
with hues of purples and blues intertwined
are not sky, but a ground
growing gardens of hospital beds,

soon-to-be graves.

No.
Not trees.
What I thought was a sturdy trunk,
I see now is powerful,
but soft.
Feathered wings
at least twice my height
Wider than Grace
which once roared above my head.

Now there are creatures coming into focus,
but their shadows keep intentions hidden.
Wings of the Bringer
of death
or salvation,
it's not my answer to give.

I can only say
what you looked like
when I pulled you out
of the line of fire,
not fast enough.

I didn't go visit
after you were taken by the medics.
Guess I'd rather face the bullets.

But I often come in my dreams.
And i see those winged creatures,
some tinged in red.
There's only one I can make out.
The one on your bed.
He's bloody.

It's at this moment that I decide
those creatures
were guardian angels.

Orienteering in Florissant, MO

Life is like a carousel.
The loud noises and bright lights,
but it's going 10 times faster
than the ones at the carnival.
And I'm constantly suffering from
motion sickness.

There are these moments, though,
fleeting moments,
where my nausea subsides
and wonder takes over.

It's when you're humping
an ATM in broad daylight.
And when your ass
is sticking out the car window
on the interstate.
It's when you look back
and see 10 spray paint tags,
which will always remind you of this day.
It's when Walmart has a bomb scare.
Because of you.

It's these moments,

orienteering through Florissant, MO
with 3 friends, a task list, and a cd,
that I breathe, feel a release,
and realize that at every turn,
the view is beautiful.

Something About Hospital Rooms

No matter how tightly I pull the privacy curtains closed,
I cant help but curse the sun for rising
even through my nightmares.

Contaminated

I'm after something pure

Pure happiness,
but no matter how happy I feel,
I'll always remember my dad screaming I'm a
slut,
and the happiness evaporates.

Pure love,
but no matter how enamored I am,
the probability of my not remembering
your touch in 5 years
Creeps in and stays in my heart.

Even pure sadness.
But no matter how many tears I shed,
my nephew's laughter lives in my eyes.

Anything pure.
But I don't think I'll ever feel it.
My heart is a quilt of red and blue squares,
pumping indecisive insecurity through my veins.

I will never know the safety of certainty,
and that, I am certain of.

Either, Or, But

I'm dancing on the fence
between condemning fate
and trying to learn the intended lesson
but with every step, my stability's at stake.

Depression

I've worn these soles
for so long I can't remember
what it feels like to walk
without the sting of pebbles
forcing their way in, staying unwelcomed.

These shoes are so comfortable,
but have laces unable to keep a knot,
frayed at the ends like a fan.
These shoes are so comfortable,
but have holes riddling the canvas
and leak the second a drop hits the ground
These shoes are so comfortable,
but when I take them off,
my feet are pruned, red and aching.

Every stitch still holding it together
is holding me together too.
Forever in this beaten up, about to break from.
But this is what I know.
So I keep walking.

Be Careful

He's such a nice guy,
and he's not known for this sort of thing.
Knew him for years - great grades,
always smiling, really going places.
He couldn't have -

And honestly, his word against hers,
isn't much of a fight.
And anyway,
ya can't be surprised
when she left her house
looking like that.

With her painted bedroom eyes,
and that cherry stain on her mouth -
even Monroe would blush.
And that skirt, grabbing her hips,
inviting eyes and hands and the rest.

She was probably drunk. And sloppy.
Can't blame him for seeing an easy score
and going for it.
And from what I hear, she wasn't complaining
while it was happening, either.
Typical slut.

At this point, ya need a damn contract
just so she won't come back
to destroy your life.
to make everyone hate you.
to make you hate yourself.
to dehumanize you.
to show you your lack of worth.
to make you a victim.

Ya gotta be careful, Man.

Proper Education

I will not teach you
to follow the rules,
only the best ways I've learned to break them.

"May I" 's will not be heard.
Only "How Can I" 's here.

No, I will not teach to the standardized test,
I teach for the unstandardized child.

I measure "proper education" as follows :
Students learning to never stop asking questions.
Progress.
They will learn to look
at everything in new ways. Up-side down ways.
Progress.
Students will learn a new language
of connection
to himself and to the world.
Progress.
Students will learn to never be satisfied with the
status quo.
Only Progress.

Faulty Forecast

A change in the weather makes me feel
unearthed.
It shows me that I am bit connected to nature
in any other sense beyond dependency.

An umbrella for rain
that I end up dragging behind me
for the dry mile - walk back home.

Arms with goosebumps
because when the weather man said 60 degrees
he really meant 40.

The suffocation of sweatpants
on a day in December that somehow feels like
July.

An annual trip to the Botanical Gardens
being downgraded to a movie day at your place
because it snows in April in Missouri.

We have no control.
Mother Nature owes us nothing,
and she reminds us every day.

Acquired Wisdom

The last poem of your first book
is a lot of pressure.
I've never been good under those conditions.

But somewhere in here,
I hope you've found a line
to aid you
in your own truth-seeking.